The Rosary:

Eucharistic Meditations

The Rosary: Eucharistic Meditations

with St. Peter Julian Eymard,
Apostle of the Eucharist

Ivonne J. Hernandez

Elisheba House
Trinity, FL

Nihil Obstat:

Rev. Monsignor David L. Toups, S.T.D.
Censor Liborum

Imprimatur:

Most Reverend Gregory L. Parkes
Bishop of St. Petersburg
November 15, 2017

Elisheba House
Trinity, Fl
www.elishebahouse.com

ISBN-13: 978-1732137707
ISBN-10: 1732137706

To Our Lady of the Blessed Sacrament

"The Holy Eucharist is Jesus Christ past, present, and future. Let the Most Holy Eucharist therefore be the starting point of our meditations on the mysteries, virtues, and truths of our religion."

St. Peter Julian Eymard

Table of Contents

Foreword

You hold in your hand a precious gift that comes to you from the inspiration of the Holy Spirit and the reflections of Ivonne Hernandez. She shares with you her story that unites in her life the love she has for God present to us in the Blessed Sacrament and her devotion to the Blessed Mother expressed in her praying the Rosary. There is a third element to be discovered in the words of this book and these come from a humble priest who was born in La Mure, France, February 4, 1811. He had a great devotion to Mary and would walk with rosary in hand on pilgrimage to visit her shrines in the French Alps.

Peter Julian Eymard claims it was Mary who led him to the priesthood, ordained in the diocese of Grenoble on July 20, 1811. After a few years of zealous pastoral ministry, he felt another tug in his soul and requested from his bishop to join the newly formed Congregation of the Marist Fathers in 1834. When you pray the rosary with a listening heart you find that Mary always leads you to her Son. It was in the Marian shrine of Fourviere that Peter Julian was again asked to leave everything behind and establish a religious congregation entirely dedicated to the love of God in the Eucharist and an apostolate of making that love known to others. It was on May 13, 1856, the feast of Our Lady of the Blessed Sacrament.

This year, 2018 marks the 150th year of his death on August 1, 1868. It is time to receive the inspiration of this Saint who was canonized at the Second Vatican Council December 9, 1962 and given the eminent title, *Apostle of the Eucharist,* by Saint Pope John, XXIII. In the legacy of St. Peter Julian is written, *"As the divine Mother of Jesus, they shall pay the highest honor in their praise and in their heart, they shall never separate the Son from the Mother, whose flesh His is."* Constitutions #78.

The *Rule of Life* for the members of the Eymardian family states, *"Mary, mother of Jesus, voice of the poor and the lowly, welcomed the Word of God into her heart and put it into practice. She shared her life and prayer with the disciples actively working with them for the coming of the Kingdom. We will honor Mary as the poor one of Yahweh and the Servant of the Lord, with a love like that of our Founder who also invoked her under the title of Our Lady of the Blessed Sacrament. We will love to meditate the mysteries of the Rosary."* #14.

You hold a gift that will transform your praying of the Rosary while reflecting on the 20 mysteries of God incarnate. The prayer will bring us to place the Eucharist at the center of our lives and live the mysteries that make known the love of God in our lives. Thank you Ivonne for this gift.

Father William Fickel, S.S.S.
Pastor, St. Vincent de Paul Catholic Church
Holiday, FL
3/25/2018

Preface

"I want you to come here on the thirteenth of next month."
My heart jolted at the sound of these words. I looked up at my friend Laura who was reading out loud the message from Our Lady of Fatima to Lucia on her June 13th apparition during our monthly prayer cell meeting, and thought to myself, "What?" And just at that moment, Laura proceeded to repeat the words: *"I want you to come here on the thirteenth of next month. I want you to continue saying the Rosary every day... I want you to learn to read and write, and later I will tell you what else I want of you."* It was Laura reading, but it was Our Lady speaking directly to my heart. You see, I had just asked Our Lady what she wanted of me. I had been discerning for months whether to be inducted, together with my husband, into the Lay Association of the Congregation of the Blessed Sacrament. The induction was scheduled for the thirteenth of next month, May 13, 2016.

I knew I had my answer, and it came directly from our Blessed Mother.

Even as I write this, a year and a half after the fact, my heart starts dancing inside my chest. The memory of this call is as vivid as it was on that day. Every fiber of my being resonated at the words from Our Lady. I imagine this is how the servers at the wedding feast at Cana felt when she told them "Do whatever He tells you." Her gentle but compelling voice removed all fear and doubts from my heart and compelled me to act. She was asking me to go to the school of the Eucharist and sign up for St. Peter Julian Eymard's class. She was asking me to become a Lay Associate of the Congregation of the Blessed Sacrament.

Our Blessed Mother had been preparing me for this moment for a while. I had made a promise to her five years earlier when I consecrated myself to Jesus through Mary on March 25, 2011, following the Total Consecration method of St. Louis de Montfort.[1] I had promised to give

---

[1] Total Consecration comes from the spiritual teaching of St. Louis Marie de Montfort, a French priest (1673-1716) who saw the need for people to grow in their relationship of love with Jesus Christ. He was inspired to understand that "the surest way" to do this was to grow in a relationship of love with the Mother of Jesus. (https://www.hbgdiocese.org/wp-content/uploads/2012/05/Consecration-to-Jesus-through-Mary-_3_-8x11.pdf)

over to Mary my whole life so I could be molded into her Divine Son using the same perfect mold God chose the first time, our Blessed Mother. My friend Laura, the same one I mentioned before, brought this devotion to our Catholic homeschool group and we prepared and consecrated as a group. The yearly renewal of my consecration promise has brought me to a deeper understanding of the mystery of giving my life over to Mary. I have learned to recognize her voice and to see her guiding hand in my life.

Wherever Mary is, her spouse the Holy Spirit is with her. And when she speaks, He comes out in her breath and brings new life. Her words to me that day were like her greeting to her cousin Elizabeth, causing my heart to leap for joy.

My husband and I were inducted to the Lay Association of the Congregation of the Blessed Sacrament on May 13, 2016. This was the 160th anniversary of Our Lady of the Blessed Sacrament, and the 99th anniversary of the feast of Our Lady of Fatima. Mary, as any good mother, knows her children very well. She knows that I always notice coincidences around dates, and she uses that to speak to me. Is it a coincidence that we had begun the formation program for the lay associates on October 13th, the anniversary of the famous *Miracle of the Sun* at Fatima, and that, while studying the messages of Our Lady of Fatima I felt her calling me to be inducted on the anniversary of her first apparition there, which just happened to be the 160th anniversary of Our Lady of the Blessed Sacrament? Maybe to others, but not to me. These dates would gain greater significance for me later, as the words "...*later I will tell you what else I want of you*" echoed in my heart.

In January of the following year, my friend Laura, who is also a Lay Associate, was preparing a new method of Consecration for our online prayer group, *Mothers of the Blessed Sacrament*. This year we would consecrate to Our Lady of the Blessed Sacrament using St. Peter Julian Eymard's spirituality, and she was planning to guide us through an online study by posting her thoughts on the readings of each day, along with themes and specific prayers for each week. This preparation was set to begin on February 13th, and conclude with our consecration on March 25th, the feast of the Annunciation. A week before we were set to begin, I felt that we needed a way to share these thoughts with a larger audience. I had a few friends who were not part of our online prayer cenacle who were interested in following along with us. Laura loved the idea, and so, on February 13, 2017, *exactly nine months* after my induction into the Lay Association, the Elisheba Blog[2] was born.

People often ask me about the name of the blog, Elisheba. It is the Hebrew form of the name Elizabeth, which means God's Promise. "All of God's promises of love announced by the prophets are fulfilled in the new and eternal covenant in his Christ" (CCC, 2787), in the Eucharist. The blog, as well as this book, are ways to fulfill my promise as a Lay Associate of the Congregation of the Blessed Sacrament: "to make known the love of God present in the Eucharist."

As we were wrapping up the posts for the Consecration to Our Lady of the Blessed Sacrament, I felt a strong inspiration to meditate on the mysteries of the Rosary from the point of view of the Eucharist, using Father Eymard's teachings, and share my reflections on the blog. There were at least two major problems with this. First, I was not comfortable with the idea of writing for the blog. I was not

---

[2] https://www.elishebahouse.com/blog

a writer after all. And second, I had been wanting to pray the Rosary regularly for a long time but sticking to routines has never been one of my areas of strength. How could I write about something I really did not know much about? I asked, "How can this be?"

And then I remembered: "*…later I will tell you what else I want of you…* do whatever He tells you." There was that gentle voice again, kindling the fire in my heart. From that fire I heard a voice that said, "My grace is sufficient for you, my power is made perfect in weakness." And my heart answered, "Let it be done to me."

The reflections compiled in this book were first published on the Elisheba Blog and now I share with you this gift that was given to me. I pray that this book helps you grow closer to the heart of Jesus in the Most Blessed Sacrament, together with our Blessed Mother, and that it may all be for the greater glory of God.

Ivonne J. Hernandez
Trinity, FL
1/25/18

Feast of the Conversion of Saint Paul, Apostle

Introduction

May Jesus be your divine center; that is my whole wish for you; a total and self-embracing center -- that is, the source of your thoughts and desires, the impulse of your actions, the basis of your love, and the measure of your sacrifices.

- St. Peter Julian Eymard

St. Peter Julian Eymard is indeed a Saint for our times. Canonized at the closing of the Second Vatican Council, his love for Jesus present in the Eucharist was the driving force in his life. The following prayer is from the liturgy on his feast day, August 2nd:

O God, You filled Saint Peter Julian with wondrous love for the mysteries of the Body and Blood of Your Son. Grant, we beseech You, that like him, we may experience the richness of this holy banquet. Grant this through our Lord Jesus Christ...[3]

Born in La Mure, France in 1811, during a time when the errors of Jansenism[4] were prevalent, he "struggled his whole life to seek that inner perfection that would enable him to offer the gift of his entire self."[5] Father Eymard eventually moved from a spirituality of reparation to one centered on the love of Christ. He saw in the Eucharist "Christ's gift of self out of love for us, waiting for our response of love to him and to our fellow human beings."[6]

Father Eymard envisioned a global Eucharistic family giving glory to Jesus in the Blessed Sacrament; a family of

---

[3] http://www.ssscongregatio.org/index.php/en/about-us/the-founder/feast-day-liturgy

[4] a religious movement which focused on the gravity of human sinfulness and a belief in the unworthiness of human motivation and activity (http://blessedsacrament.com/us/st-peter-julian-eymard)

[5] http://blessedsacrament.com/us/st-peter-julian-eymard/

[6] http://www.ssscongregatio.org/index.php/en/about-us/the-founder

priests, religious and lay people. He founded the Congregation of the Blessed Sacrament (priests and brothers) and the Congregation of the Sister Servants of the Blessed Sacrament (sisters). He believed that a fully Eucharistic life consisted of both, contemplation and apostolic activity.[7] The members of the Aggregation of the Blessed Sacrament (Associates) share in the charism of St. Peter Julian Eymard, committing themselves to be disciples and apostles of the Eucharist.

Although I had read some of St. Peter Julian's writings a few years back, it was not until my induction into the Eymardian family that I discovered the riches this Saint, whom St. John Paul II called outstanding Apostle of the Eucharist, had left for the Catholic Church. Although most of the writings from Father Eymard are in French, several of them have been translated to English and are available for consultation. His complete works can be accessed at the Congregation's website.[8]

---

[7] http://blessedsacrament.com/wp-content/uploads/2013/12/Rule-of-Life1.pdf

[8] http://www.ssscongregatio.org/index.php/en/about-us/the-founder/complete-works

Most of the quotes for this book were taken from *The Real Presence*, the first of nine volumes from the *Eymard Library*, a compilation of Father Julian's sermons arranged by topic. This book was my first introduction to St. Peter Julian's teachings, and it will always have a special place in my heart. It made me see the Eucharist in a whole new light, and kindled in my heart my love for Jesus in the Blessed Sacrament.

All the mysteries have some relation to the Eucharist, for the Eucharist completes them all. They all tend toward the Eucharist; with the help of grace we must discover what is Eucharistic in the mysteries in order to nourish our devotion toward the Most Blessed Sacrament. [9]

These words were my inspiration for the Eucharistic meditations on the mysteries of the Rosary. When we pray the Rosary, we are meditating on the mysteries of Christ's life, and St. Peter Julian's writings on the Eucharist can bring insight to our meditations on these mysteries.

---

[9] Eymard, *The Real Presence*, 291

By looking at what is Eucharistic in each mystery of the Rosary, I found quotes, mostly from *The Real Presence*, which spoke to my heart, and meditated on those. The reflections I shared were the result of those meditations, and I hope an invitation for each reader to do the same.

Look at each mystery from the point of view of the Eucharist and see where it takes you. Find your own quote to launch you into the depth of the mystery and let the Holy Spirit breathe new life into your Rosary devotion, as Our Lady brings you closer to her Divine Son.

Praying the Rosary

We must keep in mind that the Holy Eucharist is Jesus Christ past, present, and future; that the Eucharist is the last development of the Incarnation and mortal life of our Savior; that in the Eucharist Jesus Christ gives us every grace; that all truths tend to and end in the Eucharist; and that there is nothing more to be added when we have said, "The Eucharist," since it is Jesus Christ. Let the Most Holy Eucharist therefore be the starting point of our meditations on the mysteries, virtues, and truths of our religion. The Eucharist is the focal point; the truths of religion are the rays. Let us start from the focus to go to the rays. [10]

---

[10] Eymard, *The Real Presence*, 6

Teach Us How to Pray

When we pray the rosary, we allow our Mother Mary to take us by the hand and teach us the mysteries of the life of Jesus. We stop at each mystery, and as we ponder with her, she fills us with the graces we need. She asks her spouse the Holy Spirit to shower us with His gifts, with every spiritual blessing from Heaven, and she rejoices with the Most Holy Trinity as they see us growing closer to God.

When we pray each mystery, we recall with our memory the stories we have learned in the Gospels and meditate on them. What if there was a better way? What if we could go to Jesus with Our Lady and ask Him to teach us about Himself? What if we could sit in the same room with Jesus and ask Him to tell us, not only what is written in the Gospels, but His perspective on those events. If we wanted to learn about WWII, we could read a history book about the war and see pictures of the events that happened, but it would be much better if we were to sit and talk with a veteran. We could ask him not only about the facts that are recorded in history, but we could get his perspective from having *experienced* those events. He could tell us things that no one else knows. He could share the secrets of his heart with us, and we would very likely become friends.

When you share your story with someone, you share your very self, you enter into a relationship. God wants to be in relationship with us. We were made for that. Jesus gives Himself to us in Communion, but He wants even more. He wants our hearts. Jesus taught the Apostles in private. He revealed to them the secrets of His heart. We can ask Him to do the same with us. These secrets are all in the Eucharist. We can meditate on the mysteries of the Most Holy Rosary, the mysteries of Jesus' life, from the Eucharist. Jesus is truly present there, Body, Blood, Soul and Divinity. When we combine the most powerful weapon for our times, the Rosary, with the Real Presence of Our Lord in the Eucharist, we are indeed sitting in the inner room of our hearts, with Jesus and Mary. Let us then ask Our Lady of The Blessed Sacrament to grant us the graces we need to go through Him, with Him and in Him; to "start from the focus and go to the rays."[11] To open our hearts in His Presence, sit at His feet, and receive "the one thing necessary." (Lk 10:42)

---

[11] Eymard, *The Real Presence*, 6

Opening Prayers

Prayer is man's greatest virtue. All virtues are comprised in it, for all the virtues are a preparation for it and a part of it. Faith believes, hope prays, and charity begs in order to give to others; humility of heart forms the prayer, confidence speaks it, and perseverance triumphs over God Himself. Eucharistic prayer has an additional merit: it goes straight to the Heart of God like a flaming dart; it makes Jesus work, act, and relive in His Sacrament; it releases His power. The adorer does still more: he prays through Jesus Christ and shares our Lord's role as Intercessor with the Father and Divine Advocate for His redeemed brethren.[12]

---

[12] Eymard, *The Real Presence*, 13

Through Him, With Him, and In Him

The Rosary begins with the Sign of the Cross, The Apostle's Creed, an Our Father on the first large bead, and three Hail Marys on the first three small beads. These three Hail Marys are offered for an increase in the three theological virtues: faith, hope, and charity. Let us ask Our Lady to clothe us with her virtues while contemplating Jesus in the Most Blessed Sacrament.

The first virtue we pray for is faith. St. Peter Julian tells us that Jesus in the Eucharist "is the object and the means of our faith."[13] We can see Him, but He is veiled. We see bread and wine, but we KNOW it is Our Lord. We say, "I do believe, help my unbelief!" (Mk 9:24) With this assent of the will, we open ourselves to receive the gift of faith, to allow it to grow in our soul. The more time we spend in His Presence, the more our love for Him will be nurtured and grow. And the more our love grows, the more our faith will grow in turn. "The clearness of one's insight into the

---

[13] Eymard, *The Real Presence,* 102

12

Eucharist is proportioned to one's greater or lesser love and purity of life."[14]

We hope for Heaven, and while we wait, we have Heaven on Earth, our Eucharistic Lord. The Baltimore Catechism defines Heaven as "the state of everlasting life in which we see God face to face, are made like unto Him in glory, and enjoy eternal happiness."[15] In the Eucharist, we see Jesus. Though veiled to our senses, our soul can see Him, can converse with Him, and can BE with Him. "Be still and know that I am God!" (Ps 46:11) So when we want to pray for an increase in the virtue of hope, let us look at Our Lord in the Eucharist, and let us rest in Him. We rest in Him assured that His promises are true, that He is with us until the end of time.

St. Peter Julian tells us that contemplation is the source of charity and love. When we think on how to contemplate, we only need to look to our model, Our Blessed Lady, who possessed all the virtues to their maximum expression. "And Mary kept all these things, reflecting on them in her heart." (Lk 2:19) Mary was in the presence of Jesus, and

---

[14] Eymard, *The Real Presence,* 102
[15] Baltimore, *A Catechism of Christian Doctrine Book 1,* 49

she pondered, she contemplated. She opened herself up to be a vessel of God's grace to the world. She still does. When we pray a Hail Mary asking for an increase in the virtue of charity, we just need to ask our Mother to teach us how to contemplate the virtues of her Son in the Eucharist. When we connect to that source of charity and love, we allow ourselves to become a conduit, a channel of grace. Charity and love will flow from His heart to ours, and from ours to our neighbor. In contemplating Jesus in the Blessed Sacrament, we are loving God for himself and our neighbor as ourselves.

"Prayer is man's greatest virtue." [16] When we pray *through* Jesus in the Eucharist for an increase in the three theological virtues, we are in reality taking part in His prayer to the Father, *with* Him and *in* Him. We do not need to worry about whether our prayer is enough, or if we are *doing it right*. We don't even have to say anything! We just need to raise our hearts to Our Lord in the Eucharist and He will hide us within His wounds. The Father will only see His beloved Son. "If you then, who are wicked, know how to give good gifts to your children, how much more

---

[16] Eymard, *The Real Presence*, 13

will your heavenly Father give good things to those who ask him." (Mt 7:11) Let us then ask our Blessed Mother to help us to pray with the confidence of a child, and to be with us as we ask our heavenly Father, through Jesus in the Eucharist, for an increase in faith, hope and charity.

The Joyful Mysteries

1. The Annunciation

The Heart of Jesus answered that what was enough to effect the Redemption was not enough to satisfy His love; ..."I love men more than the best of mothers ever loved her child! I will stay with them . . ." "Under what form?" "Under the veiled form of the Sacrament." Divine majesty objected to such a humiliation, greater than that of the Incarnation, and more self-abasing than the Passion itself: "The salvation of man does not call for such abasement." "But," replied the Sacred Heart, "I want to veil Myself and My glory, lest the splendor of My Person prevent my poor brethren from coming to me as the glory of Moses once did the Jews. I want to throw a veil over My virtues, lest they humiliate man and incline him to despair of ever attaining so perfect a Model." He will thus come to Me more easily, and, seeing Me stoop down to the very confines of nothingness, he will come down with Me. I will have the right to say to him with more authority: "Learn of Me, that I am meek and humble of heart."[17]

---

[17] Eymard, *The Real Presence*, 38

Learn from Me

The mystery of the Annunciation speaks to us of humility. The God of the universe came down from Heaven to the womb of the Virgin, to become like us in all things but sin. To take on our humanity and weakness, to experience trials and pain, suffering and loss. The Word became flesh and dwelt among us. (Jn 1:14) Can there be a greater act of humility? Yes! That same God, who loves us more than the best of mothers ever loved her child, decided that becoming human for a time was not enough for His love; that He wanted to remain with us until the end of days. He decided He would become our food. He would strip Himself not only of His heavenly glory, but He would strip Himself of any human glory, to become bread and wine. He would come down at the call of a priest and become flesh again. Only this time, it was not as a baby in the most perfect and beautiful womb, the womb of Mary. He would come down to wherever the priest would bring Him. He knew He would suffer greater humiliations as the Eucharist than He did as a man, but that did not matter. He had but one goal in mind: communion with us. He had one desire: "Man will come down with me to the very confines of nothingness."[18] Deep calling into deep. His heart calling to our hearts. His love calling to our love. His love ever present, inviting us to union, to communion. And through that communion we would help Him become incarnate one more time, but this time in us, when we become what we eat.

---

[18] Eymard, *The Real Presence*, 38

2. The Visitation

She (Mary) eagerly sacrificed her privacy and the sweetness of contemplation, in order to go to her cousin Elizabeth, to felicitate her and to serve her. ...Mary did not receive the Word for herself alone. She rejoiced that we should be able to participate in her happiness. Let us, then, unite ourselves with her when we receive Jesus. Let us sing her Magnificat. The Lord, in this mystery, has done great things in Mary; and He has also done great things in coming to us. Let us strive to imitate her virtues so that Jesus Christ may find in us, as in His holy Mother, a dwelling worthy of Him. [19]

"The Eucharist is a burning coal, which sets us on fire." Fire is active by nature and tends to spread. When the soul is under the action of the Eucharist, it is forced to cry out: "O my God, what shall I do in return for so much love?" And Jesus answers: "Thou hast to resemble Me, to live for Me, and to live off Me." The transformation will be easy; when it is a matter of love, says the Imitation of Christ, one does not walk; one runs and flies. [20]

---

[19] Eymard, *Our Lady of The Blessed Sacrament*, 59
[20] Eymard, *The Real Presence*, 262

Live off Me

The mystery of the Visitation speaks to us of love of neighbor or charity. Why did Mary make haste to visit her cousin? She had just had the most amazing encounter with the Holy Spirit. She had Jesus dwelling in her. Why didn't she take some time to enjoy the moment, to take it all in? Precisely because she had Jesus dwelling in her. They became one. His wishes became her wishes. His love became her love. Her joy was such that it had to be shared. Mary did not have to choose between contemplating the mystery of God dwelling within her and loving her neighbor, and neither do we. We do not receive Jesus only for ourselves. He wants us to take Him to all those who can't or won't go to Him.

St. Peter Julian tells us that "the Eucharist is a burning coal, which sets us on fire."[21] This is the fire of God's love, which burns but doesn't consume and wants to spread like a wildfire. "I have come to set the earth on fire, and how I wish it were already blazing!" (Lk 12:49) If we let it, this

---

[21] Eymard, *The Real Presence*, 262

fire will transform us into Himself. We will become one with Him and will burn with His love. Just like Mary, we will hasten to our neighbor. We will bring Jesus everywhere we go and will sing his praises as we join our Mother singing her Magnificat, for the Lord has indeed done great things for us. When we let the fire of the love of God animate our lives, we grow perfect in charity. It is in this moment where true contemplation lives. Our life becomes a living prayer and we become God's hands and feet in the world.

3. The Nativity

When He was born on the straw of the stable, the Word was preparing His Eucharist, which He considered the complement of all His other mysteries. He was coming to be united to man. During His life He would establish with man a union of grace, a union of example and of merit; but only in the Eucharist would He consummate the most perfect union of which man is capable here below. ...

This heavenly wheat was as it were sown at Bethlehem, the "House of bread." See the wheat on the straw. Trodden down and crushed, this straw represents poor humanity. Of itself it is barren. But Jesus will lift it into position in Himself, will restore it to life, and will make it fruitful.[22]

---

[22] Eymard, *The Real Presence*, 237

Be Still

The mystery of the Nativity speaks to us of poverty and vulnerability. In the stillness of the night, Our Savior was born in a manger, a poor infant, completely vulnerable and dependent upon His parents. By the manner of His birth at Bethlehem, He teaches us detachment from all earthly things, not only in material possessions, but also in spirit. In the Eucharist, Jesus continues to teach us the lessons we need to prepare the way of the Lord, so He can be born in our hearts.

Jesus is poorer and more vulnerable in the Eucharist than He was at Bethlehem. He depends on man for everything, from the matter of His sacrifice, to the linens and the candles for His altars. [23] He makes Himself vulnerable out of love. When we see Him in that state, we feel we can approach Him. We see ourselves in the mirror of the Host and realize it is okay to allow ourselves to be vulnerable with Him. We open our hearts and show Him

---

[23] Eymard, *The Real Presence*, 132

our nothingness, our poverty, our brokenness. "A contrite, humbled heart, O God, you will not scorn." (Ps 51:19)

Just like the straw was "trodden down and crushed,"[24] so our hearts, crushed by our sin, will become the poor bed our Lord seeks. "Be still and know that I am God!" (Ps 46:11) In the stillness of our hearts, our Lord will be born. He will bring with Him the infant virtues we need to grow. We will nourish them with the Bread of Life and water them with Living Water. Each time we receive Our Lord there will be less of us and more of Him. We will declare with John the Baptist, "He must increase; I must decrease" (Jn 3:30), until we can one day say, "I live, no longer I, but Christ lives in me!" (Gal 2:20)

---

[24] Eymard, *The Real Presence*, 237

4. The Presentation

Our Lord would not delay to offer Himself publicly to His Father. Forty days after His Birth, He inspired Mary to take Him to the Temple. Mary carried her Infant in her arms, about to offer Him to the Father, and to buy Him back with two turtle-doves. Jesus willed to be purchased for these little creatures, which speak to us of His purity and simplicity.[25]

(In the Eucharist) He obeys not only at Mass when the priest pronounces the words of the consecration, but at every moment of the day and night, whenever the faithful need Him. His permanent state is one of genuine and simple obedience.[26]

---

[25] Eymard, *Our Lady of The Blessed Sacrament*, 72
[26] Eymard, *The Real Presence*, 61

Listen to Me

The mystery of the Presentation of Jesus in the Temple speaks to us of obedience. "He inspired Mary to take Him to the Temple."[27] Mary's steps were inspired by Jesus, who had, even as an infant, only His Father's will in mind. He wanted to offer himself publicly to His Father, and, at the same time, teach us about purity and simplicity.

Why was Jesus so eager to start teaching us about purity? Perhaps it is because purity of heart is a requirement for the beatific vision, which is our ultimate goal. "Blessed are the pure in heart, for they shall see God." (Mt 5:8) St. Peter Julian tells us that "the clearness of one's insight into the Eucharist is proportioned to one's greater or lesser love and purity of life."[28] We are not pure enough to see through the Eucharistic veil on our own. We need Mary, our Mother and perfect model, to help us. We need to ask her, with the simplicity of a child, to clothe us with her virtues so we can sit at the feet of Our Lord and learn from Him. The pure of heart can pierce through the Eucharistic veil

---

[27] Eymard, *Our Lady of The Blessed Sacrament*, 72
[28] Eymard, *The Real Presence*, 102

and contemplate our Lord now, in this Heaven on earth,[29] as we wait in hope for the day when we see Him with unveiled faces. In that contemplation, we will hear His inspirations.

When I think of Mary carrying the infant Jesus and presenting Him at the Temple, a story our parish priest once shared comes to mind. He said that one day, as he was carrying the Monstrance to the teens during Eucharistic Adoration, he heard Jesus tell him: "Just take me to where I need to go, and I'll do the rest." Jesus was inspiring his steps just like He inspired Mary's. As an infant He couldn't walk to the Temple to offer Himself to the Father. He needed Mary. In the Eucharist He can't get to where He needs to go by himself. He needs man. He needs the priest to bring Him to the altar, to bring Him to the sick, to bring Him to those who want to receive Him, and He needs us to bring Him to the rest of the world. Let us grow in purity and simplicity, so we can listen to the inspirations of Jesus in the Eucharist. We can then let Him guide our steps, and bring us with Him, in obedience, to the will of the Father.

---

[29] Eymard, *Our Lady of The Blessed Sacrament*, 26

5. Finding of Jesus in the Temple

Our Lord in the Blessed Sacrament is His own Light, His own means of being known, just as the sun is itself its own proof. To make Himself known, He has only to show Himself. We need not resort to reasoning to understand that; a child does not have to discourse with itself to recognize its parents. Our Lord manifests Himself through the reality of His presence as parents do. ... He speaks only one word, but a word that rings in our very hearts: "It is I! . . ." And we sense His presence, we believe in it more firmly than if we were to see Him with our eyes. [30]

---

[30] Eymard, *The Real Presence*, 191

Remain in Me

The mystery of the Finding of Jesus in the Temple speaks to us of devotion. Devotion keeps us coming back to the practices we know will bring us closer to God, even when we feel we have lost Him. When Mary and Joseph lost sight of Jesus they were filled with anxiety and worry. We too lose sight of Jesus in our lives. Often, we let ourselves get carried away by the cares of life, and when we look back, we realize Jesus is not with us anymore. We think He is lost, that He left us, but it is we who are lost. It is we who turned our eyes towards something else. It is at those times that devotion to the Blessed Sacrament will be our saving grace.

It is in the reality of the Real Presence of Jesus in the Most Blessed Sacrament that we will find ourselves. Only through that light of Truth will we be able to see our hearts the way God sees us. As we contemplate Jesus in His own light, He will reveal ourselves to us. He will reveal the areas that are distracting us from following Him. We will be able to see our nothingness, and not be afraid, because He is veiled in nothingness Himself. He will draw us to Himself and speak to our hearts. We will find ourselves in Him, because He is the Way.

Mary and Joseph eventually found Jesus in the Temple. After they found Him, they brought Him home and He stayed with them. Jesus wants to remain with us always. We must do everything in our power to remain in His presence. "Remain in me, as I remain in you. Just as a branch cannot bear fruit on its own unless it remains on the vine, so neither can you unless you remain in me." (Jn 15:4) We need the Eucharist, which is our daily bread. St. Peter Julian calls love for the Most Blessed Sacrament, the "mother and queen of all other devotions and the sunlight of piety."[31] This devotion will be our sustenance for the road. When our hearts are filled with fear and anxiety because we can't see Jesus, we need but to turn our eyes towards Jesus in the Most Blessed Sacrament. St. Peter Julian tells us that:

Our Lord sees as far as your home; He listens to you from His tabernacle. He can see us from Heaven; why could He not see us from the Sacred Host? Adore Him from where you are; you

---

[31] Eymard, *The Real Presence*, 315

will make a good adoration of love, and our Lord will understand your desire.[32]

Let us then turn our eyes towards Jesus in the Most Blessed Sacrament, and listen as he whispers in our hearts, "It is I!"

---

[32] Eymard, *The Real Presence*, 319

The Mysteries of Light

1. The Baptism of the Lord

In the Eucharist we find a remedy for our ills, and a payment for the fresh debts we contract daily towards Divine justice through our sins. Our Lord offers Himself up every morning as a Victim of propitiation for all the sins of the world.[33]

Propitiation consists in making amends to our Lord and in consoling Him. That is what our mission as adorers largely consists in. We ought to make reparation; we ought to be mediators and penitents for the sins of men. The world is so wicked that there is almost greater need of reparation than of thanksgiving. John made reparation when he said: "Behold the Lamb of God, behold Him Who takes away the sin of the world." He preached and showed the atoning Victim. He wept and sorrowed over the indifference of men toward the Savior. Listen to his complaint: "There has stood One in the midst of you, Whom you know not."[34]

---

[33] Eymard, *The Real Presence*, 143
[34] Ibid., 301

Behold

The mystery of the Baptism of Jesus in the River Jordan speaks to us of reparation. The beloved Son of the Father opened up the fountain of Baptism for us by His death on the Cross. "Behold, the Lamb of God, behold Him Who takes away the sin of the world."[35] These words from John the Baptist are repeated at every Mass as the priest elevates the Eucharist. "Christ's sacrifice present on the altar makes it possible for all generations of Christians to be united with his offering."[36] Let us then offer Jesus in the Blessed Sacrament our adoration in reparation for our sins and those of the whole world.

"The world is so wicked there is almost greater need of reparation than of thanksgiving."[37] These words from St. Peter Julian remind us that we can and must unite our offerings to those of Christ. "The law entered in so that transgression might increase but, where sin increased, grace overflowed all the more." (Rom 5:20) When we unite our

---

[35] http://www.catholic-resources.org/ChurchDocs/CatholicMass-BasicTexts-Rev3.pdf
[36] (CCC, 1368)
[37] Eymard, *The Real Presence*, 301

lives to the sacrifice of Christ, our works, prayers, suffering and praise take on new value. They are now, infinite in the power of God, the vehicle of that grace that will overflow where sin abounds. Evil and darkness are but the absence of good and light. God has placed each of us in our lives at precisely the time and place He needs us, so we can bring His light to the places that are still in darkness. By uniting every aspect of our lives with the Eucharist, we fulfill our priestly duties, received through Baptism, to sanctify the world and offer sacrifice to God.

We are all sinners, and in the Eucharist, "we find a remedy for our ills, and a payment for the fresh debts we contract daily towards Divine justice through our sins."[38] By acknowledging our sinfulness and repenting, we are able to receive forgiveness, but after our sins are forgiven justice still demands reparation. The Catechism tells us that "the expiation of sins continues in the mystical body of Christ and the communion of saints by joining our human acts of atonement to the redemptive action of Christ, both in this life and in Purgatory."[39] Let us then adore and console our Lord in the Eucharist, the One the world does

---

[38] Eymard, *The Real Presence*, 143
[39] CCC, location 27720 of 28417

not know. Let us unite our voices to John the Baptist and say Behold!

2. The Wedding Feast at Cana

Why is our Lord not my center? Because He is not yet the ego of my ego, because I am not completely under His control, under the inspiration of His will; because I have desires that are competing with the desires of Jesus within me; because He does not mean everything to me. ... What am I to do? I must enter into this center, abide in it, and act in it, not indeed by the sentiment of His sweetness, which does not depend on me, but by repeated attempts, by the homage of every action. ... Abide in our Lord. Abide in Him through a sense of devotedness, of holy joy, of readiness to do whatever He will ask of you. Abide in the Heart and the peace of Jesus Eucharistic. [40]

---

[40] Eymard, *The Real Presence*, 138

Hear My Voice

The mystery of the Wedding Feast at Cana speaks to us of our free will. "Do whatever He tells you." (Jn 2:5) These words from Mary to the servants at the wedding echo in our hearts today. They present to us a challenge and a choice. "And when I am lifted up from the earth, I will draw everyone to myself." (Jn 12:32) From the Host as from the Cross, He is always drawing us to Himself, drawing us near "to bind us with the chains of His love,"[41] and to fill us with His peace. It is up to us to accept His invitation, to make the Eucharist the center of our lives and to follow Him.

Only the true center of the universe can draw all things to Himself. Just like the planets revolve around the sun and are held in its path by gravity, whatever we place at the center of our lives will pull us in its direction and influence our path. When we choose other goods over the supreme good, we are in reality worshiping false gods, like the god of money, the god of honor, the god of power, or the god

---

[41] Eymard, *The Real Presence*, 179

of self. These lesser *gods* will pull us away from the path God chose for us, not because they are stronger in themselves, but because as we grow closer to them we distance ourselves from God. The nearer we draw to the Eucharist, the stronger we will feel its pull, and the less power these other *gods* will have over us. We must make Our Eucharistic Lord the center of our lives and we "must enter into this center, abide in it, and act in it."[42]

To abide in our Lord is an act of the will. We must repeatedly strive to grow in virtue, follow the teachings of our Mother Church, and frequent the sacraments. This is especially important during those times when we do not feel the sweetness of consolation. The enemy of our souls will continually try to lure us with other goods and with promises of temporary relief and consolation, but we must "hold unwaveringly to our confession that gives us hope, for he who made the promise is trustworthy." (Heb 10:23) We must remain close to Jesus in the Blessed Sacrament, receive Him often and spend time with Him. He will then draw us to Himself with the chains of His love and fill us with His peace. We will learn to recognize His sweet voice

---

[42] Eymard, *The Real Presence*, 138

and we will want nothing more than to follow our Mother's instructions and do whatever He tells us. He will then smile and say, "My sheep hear my voice; I know them, and they follow me." (Jn 10:2)

3. The Proclamation of the Kingdom

All graces come from the Host. From His Eucharist Jesus sanctifies the world, but in an invisible and spiritual manner. He rules the world and the Church without either moving or speaking. Such must the kingdom of Jesus be in me, all interior. I must gather myself up around Jesus: my faculties, my understanding, and my will; and my senses, as far as possible. I must live of Jesus and not of myself, in Jesus and not in myself. I must pray with Him, immolate myself with Him, and be consumed in the same love with Him. I must become in Him one flame, one heart, one life with Him. ...This life in Jesus is nothing other than the love of predilection, the gift of self, the intensifying of union with Him; through it we take root, as it were, and prepare the nourishment, the sap of the tree. The kingdom of God is within you. [43]

---

[43] Eymard, *The Real Presence*, 139

Remain in Me

The mystery of the Proclamation of the Kingdom speaks to us of our center, our hearts. The Catechism tells us that "the desire for God is written in the human heart, because man is created by God and for God; and God never ceases to draw man to himself." (CCC, 27) This same Word, Who was written in our hearts before the foundation of the world, was made flesh, dwelt among us, and continues to dwell among us in the Eucharistic kingdom of our hearts.

Before the foundation of the world, God held each of our hearts in His hand and wrote in them the name of His beloved Son, marking us as His chosen people. This Word was etched in our hearts with the indelible ink of the Blood of the Lamb and sealed with the fire of the Holy Spirit. It is our center, our true identity. The Catechism tells us that "the heart is our hidden center, beyond the grasp of our reason and of others; only the Spirit of God can fathom the human heart and know it fully." (CCC, 2563) We all have a desire, a need to be known. Our hearts are restless, searching to be fulfilled.

Who am I? I am a mother, a daughter, a sister, a friend. We define our identity in relation to others. It is through the mirror of a loving parent's eyes that an infant knows she is loved and cherished. Since we are each made in the image of God, we should be able to reflect God to each other, but our mirrors have become distorted through sin. We walk through life as if through a house of mirrors, where we seem too tall, too short, too fat, or too skinny. We look at our neighbor through the same mirrors and their reflection is distorted too.

It is only in the mirror of the Eucharist that we will find our true identity. It is here where we will hear the Truth spoken to our hearts. "You formed my inmost being; you knit me in my mother's womb." (Ps 139) It is in that truth we will find rest and in union with Him that the kingdom of God will take root in our hearts. "I made known to them your name and I will make it known, that the love with which you loved me may be in them and I in them." (Jn 17:26)

4. The Transfiguration

Whereas on Tabor Jesus had rent the veil that covered His Divinity, here He conceals even His humanity and transfigures it into the appearances of bread, to the point that He no longer seems to be either God or Man, and does not act outwardly anymore. He buries Himself in the Species, which become the tomb of His faculties. Out of humility He veils His humanity which is so kind and beautiful. He is so united to the accidents that He seems to be their substance. The bread and wine have been changed into the Body and Blood of the Son of God. Do you see Him in this transfiguration of love and humility? We know that the sun exists even though a cloud hides it from us. Jesus never ceases being God and perfect Man, although hidden behind the cloud of bread and wine. Just as everything was glorious in the first transfiguration, so in the second everything is lovable. We see Him no longer, nor do we touch Him, but He is there with all His gifts. Love, grace, and faith pierce the veils and can recognize His face. Faith is the eye of the soul; to believe is really to see.[44]

---

[44] Eymard, *The Real Presence*, 293

Be Not Afraid

The mystery of the Transfiguration speaks to us of transformation. The verb to transfigure is defined in the dictionary as to "transform outwardly and usually for the better."[45] It is easy to see that in the Transfiguration of Jesus on Mount Tabor, where He revealed His glory, there was an outward change for the better. St. Peter Julian tells us that in the Eucharist Jesus "transfigures even His humanity into the appearances of bread."[46] How is this change for the better? Jesus always preferred humility to glory because His goal is to bring us near Him. If we look with the eyes of faith, we can see that this "transfiguration of love and humility"[47] is the greatest transformation of all. We can draw near to Him now, so near as to consume Him, thus beginning our own transformation into Himself.

In Matthew's account of the Transfiguration, we hear that the disciples "fell prostrate and were very much afraid. But Jesus came and touched them, saying, 'Rise, and do

---

[45] https://www.merriam-webster.com/dictionary/transfigure, 4/23/17
[46] Eymard, *The Real Presence*, 293
[47] Ibid.

not be afraid.'" (Mt 17:6) Jesus put aside His glory once again to come down and take care of their needs. This is what He does every day on the altar. He comes down to us, no matter how far down we have fallen, to heal us with His touch and to take away our fear. It is in the Eucharist where He brings "every spiritual blessing in the Heavens" (Eph 1:3) wrapped in a humble lovable package. He brings us the gift of Himself. We just need to look with the eye of faith and we will see His face.

The goal of this transfiguration is our own transformation. We are so thirsty for the glory of Heaven that often we are easily deceived and settle for less. We will go after anything that sparkles in the desert only to find it was all just a mirage. The fountain of living water is hidden, buried down deep in the well of the species in the Eucharist. It is here where our thirst will be quenched. When we remain hidden in this well of love, we will be transformed ourselves, and we will say with Peter, "Lord, it is good that we are here." (Mt 17:4)

5. The Institution of the Eucharist

ON THAT day, then, our Lord remembered that He was a father, and He wanted to make His will; He was about to die. What a solemn act this is in a family! It is, so to speak, the last act of one's life, and one that extends beyond the grave. A father gives what he has. He cannot give himself because he does not belong to himself. He bequeaths something to each of his children as well as to his friends. He gives what he prizes the most. But our Lord would give His very Self!

He became bread; His Body, Blood, Soul and Divinity took the place of the substance of the bread which was offered up. We do not see Him, but we have Him. Our Lord Jesus Christ is our inheritance. He wants to give Himself to everybody, but not everybody wants Him. There are some who would want Him, but they will not submit to the conditions of good and pure living which He has laid down; and their malice has the power to render God's bequest null and void.[48]

---

[48] Eymard, *The Real Presence*, 32

You Are Mine

The mystery of the Institution of the Eucharist speaks to us of our dignity as children of God. In the Eucharist Jesus left us both a new covenant and a new testament in His Blood. By the New Covenant in His Blood Christ restored our relationship with the Father, and in His last will and testament He left us the total gift of Himself in the Eucharist. It is by accepting this gift and by entering into a personal relationship with God that we can transcend the likeness of our earthly parentage and be transformed into the likeness of Our Heavenly Father.

"Our Lord remembered He was a father." [49] These words from St. Peter Julian invite us to see Jesus in a new light. In the Eucharist we have our God, Lord, friend, brother, teacher and spouse, but father? Jesus answers, "If you know me, then you will also know my Father. From now on you do know him and have seen him." (Jn 14:7) Jesus brings every heavenly grace with Him in the Eucharist; He brings us the Father and the Holy Spirit, who

---

[49] Eymard, *The Real Presence*, 32

are always dwelling in Him. We are invited to enter into this heavenly relationship, to be caught between the gaze of the Father and the Son, in the embrace of the Holy Spirit. "The dignity of man rests above all on the fact that he is called to communion with God." (CCC, 27)

"I will be a father to you, and you shall be sons and daughters to me." (2 Cor 6:18) This is what God tells us from the Eucharist. He gives Himself completely to us, and His desire is that we give ourselves completely to Him in return. During the Last Supper, Jesus prays "that they may all be one, as you, Father, are in me and I in you, that they also may be in us." (Jn 17:21) This is His will for us. He wants to heal the wounds from our earthly parentage, and restore us in our dignity as children of God. When we receive Jesus in the Most Blessed Sacrament and let Him speak to our hearts, we can hear the truth of who we are. "I have called you by name: you are mine." (Is 43:1)

The Sorrowful Mysteries

1. The Agony in the Garden

The agony of the Garden of Olives was already upon Him. At Gethsemane, Jesus would be saddened unto death at the sight of the ignominies in store for Him in His Passion. ...But now, at the Last Supper, what a struggle went on in the Heart of Jesus! What anguish! ...The Heart of Jesus was certainly not wavering, nor did it hesitate; but it was tormented. He saw His Passion renewed every day in His Sacrament of love... What was He to do? He would give Himself. He would give Himself just the same. [50]

He knew beforehand the lukewarmness of His followers: He knew mine; He knew what little fruit we would derive from Holy Communion. But He wanted to love just the same, to love more than He was loved, more than man could make return for. [51]

---

[50] Eymard, *The Real Presence*, 40
[51] Ibid., 152

Come

The mystery of the Agony in the Garden speaks to us of true contrition. When we meditate on the agony and suffering of Our Lord, our hearts open up to empathy. We see Jesus suffering deeply in His humanity, to the point of death, and upon realizing that we are the cause of such pain, we are moved to true contrition, a "sorrow of the soul and detestation for the sin committed, together with the resolution not to sin again." (CCC, 1451) His grace keeps us from falling into despair and holds us up as we see the reality of our sin. With one word from His Sacred Heart, hidden in the Sacred Host, our hearts are pierced and mercy flows. Mourning is turned into dancing and with grateful hearts we praise and adore Him.

St. Peter Julian tells us that the agony of Our Lord began at the Last Supper. It was at that moment, the one He had been eagerly awaiting, that He saw how He would be treated in the Blessed Sacrament and His heart was tormented. He saw how many hearts would not love Him. He saw how many Judases would betray Him, how many Peters would deny Him. "He knew beforehand the lukewarmness of His followers: He knew mine."[52] Jesus knew all He would suffer, but He chose to give Himself anyway. His love for us is greater than our sin. In the Blessed Sacrament, He waits patiently for us to come and weep at His feet. He wants us to go to Him with the simplicity of a child.

One time one of my boys did something that made me really sad. He was feeling ashamed and disappointed at his behavior, but when he saw I was sad, he ran to me, hugged me, said he was sorry, that he wouldn't do it again, and then he begged me to please not be sad anymore. The pain of hurting me was stronger than the shame of having broken the rules. Love was greater than his fear and he sought to console my heart. My heart was moved and we just hugged and wept. No more words were needed. Our hearts were speaking in the silence and in the tears. When we run to Jesus in the Most Blessed Sacrament with a contrite heart, when we finally return love for His love, all the pain and suffering melts away, and only love remains.

---

[52] Eymard, *The Real Presence*, 152

2. The Scourging at the Pillar

The Eucharist is the Divine lightning rod that wards off the thunderbolts of Divine Justice. As a tender and devoted mother presses her child to her bosom, puts her arms around it, and shields it with her body to save it from the wrath of an angry father, so Jesus multiplies His presence everywhere, covers the world and envelops it with His merciful presence. Divine Justice does not know then where to strike; it dares not.[53]

---

[53] Eymard, *The Real Presence*, 158

Take and Drink

The mystery of the Scourging at the Pillar speaks to us of forbearance, an extraordinarily patient endurance under provocation. With extraordinary patience, Jesus endured His Passion out of love for us. Bound to the pillar, He willingly took on the punishment for us, atoning for our sins and teaching us by His example. In the Eucharist He continues to be an example of forbearance for us. Bound to the bread and wine He waits for us, continually interceding to the Father on our behalf, until the end of time.

Amid the blows life throws at us, and the scourging caused by our own sins, we faintly remember that "my help comes from the Lord." (Ps 121:2) When the pain is too much and we feel we are about to faint, amid the blows and the blood we seek His face and pray, Lord, "Hide me in the shadow of your wings!" (Ps 17:8)

The blows keep coming, but now we are shielded by His Body. He covers us with Himself so we can regain our strength. We see His beautiful face, loving us as He grimaces in pain. He is glad to suffer for us, to teach us what to do. He tells us to drink His blood, the one dripping from His wounds. Inebriated with this cup we'll say, "But you have given my heart more joy than they have when grain and wine abound." (Ps 4:8) With this gladness now we see what we must do. We have the grace to endure too. We take our place like Him, over our neighbor who is feeling weak. We pass the cup with love and say, take and drink, this is the blood He shed for you.

3. *The Crowning with Thorns*

The honor paid to a friend in disguise, or to a king without his royal insignia, is greater than any other, because it is really the person who is then honored and not his trappings. So it goes with Jesus in the Most Blessed Sacrament; to honor Him, to believe in His Divinity in spite of the veil of weakness thrown over Him is to honor His Divine Person and to respect the mystery which envelops Him. [54]

In union with the four and twenty ancients who cast their crowns in homage at the feet of the Lamb, lay your whole being, your faculties, and all your works in homage at the foot of the Eucharistic throne and say to our Lord: "To Thee alone be love and glory! ... Holy Church entrusts this God to you that you may be her representative at His feet; offer Him her adoration." [55]

---

[54] Eymard, *The Real Presence*, 53
[55] Ibid., 8

Do You Love Me?

The mystery of the Crowning with Thorns speaks to us of courage. "He was spurned and avoided by men, a man of suffering, knowing pain." (Is 53:3) When we look at Jesus crowned with thorns, we see a contradiction; we see a man of sorrows, not a king. That contradiction is still present today in the Most Blessed Sacrament. The "veil of weakness thrown over Him"[56] makes us not recognize His face. If we had been in that room when Our Lord was being mocked and spat upon, would we have had the courage to honor Him as our King? Do we have the courage to honor Him today in the Eucharist?

One of the effects of the Sacrament of Confirmation is that "it gives us a special strength of the Holy Spirit to spread and defend the faith by word and action as true witnesses of Christ, to confess the name of Christ boldly, and never to be ashamed of the Cross." (CCC, 1304) In the contradiction of the Blessed Sacrament, we are presented with a challenge: either He is Who He says He is, or He is

---

[56] Eymard, *The Real Presence*, 53

not. If we believe He is our King, then we must give Him homage. We must never be ashamed of the Cross.

One time during Eucharistic Adoration, I was sitting in the back of the dimly lit church. Incense filled the room as it rose up in the glow of the altar candles. As I moved my eyes down from the monstrance I saw a figure on the floor. It was the priest, prostrated before the Lamb, like he had been during his priestly ordination. This sight touched me deeply. The reality before me became clear, as he boldly proclaimed the name of Jesus with his actions. I wanted to lay myself at the feet of Jesus too, but I was afraid. What would people think? Would I be able to get up gracefully from the floor? Would I make a fool of myself? While I struggled with all these questions in my heart, the time for Adoration ended, and I left a little sad. The desire to prostrate myself in front of the Most Blessed Sacrament did not leave me, and eventually, months later, God gave me the courage to follow through on that desire and it was truly a moment of grace. We don't have to physically lay ourselves down before the Eucharist to cast our crowns in homage, but we can ask for the courage to proclaim with our whole being, "To Thee alone be love and glory!"[57]

---

[57] Eymard, *The Real Presence*, 8

4. *The Carrying of the Cross*

I am the way, and the truth, and the life. (Jn 14:6) OUR Lord uttered these words while He was still among men, but He meant them to reach far beyond the short span of His human life. They belong to all ages; He can still repeat them in the Blessed Sacrament with as much truth as in Judea. ...In the Eucharist He no longer performs the acts of virtues, but He has assumed them as His form of existence. We must make the acts and thus, in a way, complete our Lord. He thereby becomes one mystical person with us. We are His acting members, His Body, of which He is the Head and the Heart; so that He can say, "I still live." We complete and perpetuate Him.[58]

---

[58] Eymard, *The Real Presence*, 187

Follow Me

The mystery of the Carrying of the Cross shows us the way we are to follow if we are to be true disciples of Christ. From embracing the Cross upon receiving it, to continuing all the way through the *Via Dolorosa* to Calvary, Our Lord exhibits all the virtues needed to reach the goal. He still exhibits them all in the Eucharist, so we can learn from Him and, as His mystical body, "complete and perpetuate Him."[59]

"Whoever wishes to come after me must deny himself, take up his cross, and follow me." (Mt 16:24) These words from Jesus leave us with a very clear map of how we are to find the treasure of Heaven. The path goes straight though the *Via Dolorosa*, which means the way of suffering. We are not only to follow Him there, but we are to do it as we carry our own daily cross. Every morning when we see our cross, we are to embrace it like He did, for it is our key to the kingdom. Each time we fall, we'll see Our Lady right there with us, and with her help, we will get up again. Sometimes

---

[59] Eymard, *The Real Presence*, 187

a Simon of Cyrene or a Veronica will come along our way, and sometimes we will be the ones called to ease someone else's way. We will be mocked and insulted; we will grow tired and wonder if we can go on; blood and sweat will stream down our eyes. We won't see Jesus in front of us and we'll wonder if He's still with us.

Jesus knew our weakness and how difficult we would find it to follow this path, so not only is He leading us by going through it ahead of us, but He left Himself behind in the Eucharist as our nourishment and guide. From there He speaks to our hearts, "I am the way, and the truth, and the life." (Jn 14:6) See how meek He is in the Eucharist, hidden and silent. Be meek like Him. See how He patiently waits for us to realize that there is something greater there, that He is everything we need. Be patient like Him. See how poor, gentle, strong, faithful, self-giving, and loving He is. Be like Him. He wants us to receive Him and become one with Him, so that when we are carrying our cross, it is He in us who is carrying it for us. With Him acting in us, and us acting in Him, we unite our sufferings to His, completing and perpetuating Him. We will say with St. Paul, "Now I rejoice in my sufferings for your sake, and in my flesh I am filling up what is lacking in the afflictions of Christ on behalf of his body, which is the church." (Col 1:24)

5. *The Crucifixion*

The Eucharist, in fact, is the fruit of the death of Jesus. The Eucharist is a testament, a legacy, which becomes valid only at the death of the testator. To give His testament legal force, Jesus had then to die. Every time we come into the presence of the Eucharist we may therefore say: This precious testament cost Jesus Christ His life; He thereby shows us His boundless love, for He Himself said there is no greater proof of love than to lay down one's life for one's friends.[60]

---

[60] Eymard, *The Real Presence*, 67

Show Me Your Wounds

The mystery of the Crucifixion speaks to us of the virtue of fortitude. The Catechism tells us that "the virtue of fortitude enables one to conquer fear, even fear of death, and to face trials and persecutions." (CCC, 1808) When we look at the sacrifice on the Cross from the point of view of the Eucharist, we see the end before our eyes. We can then look at the Cross with hope and not despair.

We go to the Eucharist, the living proof of His love, and we ask Him to show us the Way to Himself. He shows us the Cross. He shows us His glorified wounds, the fount of mercy by which our wounds are healed; we see them and remember the price He paid for them. We see how much He suffered for love of us. We touch His wounds and exclaim with St. Thomas, "my Lord and my God!" (Jn 20:28) We see Christ's death as the price paid for the gift of Himself in the Eucharist, and our hearts are moved to gratitude. Gratitude moves us to want to give Him something in return, but what can we give Him? We only have our brokenness. We show him our own wounds and pain. For this He waited. He touches our wounds and hides them within His; transforming them with His love and driving away all fear. We are united through the pain in a deep embrace of love. We find sweetness on the cross, the sweetness of being one with Him. Our pain is still there, but we are not alone and we are not afraid.

With fear now gone, we can see our suffering in the light of the Eucharist. We see that it is by uniting our wounds to His wounds that we find the pathway by which mercy will flow from Him to us, and from us to others. It is in the Eucharist, His last will and testament to us, that we find the strength we need to die to our own will and accept the sufferings that come our way.

The Glorious Mysteries

1. *The Resurrection*

It is true that the glory of the Saints and of the blessed is a flower that blooms only in the sunshine of Paradise and in the presence of God. This dazzling glory cannot be ours on this earth; people would offer us adoration. But we receive the hidden seed of it which contains it in its entirety as the seed contains the ear of wheat. The Eucharist deposits in us the leaven of resurrection, the source of a special and brighter glory, which after having been sown in our corruptible flesh will shine in our risen and immortal body.[61]

The last (effect of the Eucharist) is to make us share in His glorious Resurrection. Jesus Christ sows the seed of His own life in us; the Holy Ghost will quicken it and through it will give us a new life, but a life of glory that will never end.[62]

---

[61] Eymard, *The Real Presence*, 288
[62] Ibid., 68

Believe in Me

The mystery of the Resurrection speaks to us of faith. We see in the Risen Christ the promise that we will rise up with Him one day, and in the Eucharist we receive the seed of that promise, of a life of glory that will never end.

"The Eucharist deposits in us the leaven of resurrection." [63] Leaven is a pervasive presence that permeates everything, transforming it into something better. [64] The Eucharist, being the Risen Lord Himself, sows the seed of His own life in us, transforming us until we become what we eat.

We need to look for that little germinating plant in each other, amid the weeds in the garden, and be careful not to trample on it. We need to look for the saints God has placed in our lives, those whose flower is not yet in full bloom, but that might need our help to fertilize and tend to their garden. Helping one another to grow in holiness as we remain close to the Eucharist and encouraging one another,

---

[63] Eymard, *The Real Presence*, 288

[64] https://en.oxforddictionaries.com/definition/leaven

we will then join St. Paul when he says: "All of us, gazing with unveiled face on the glory of the Lord, are being transformed into the same image from glory to glory, as from the Lord who is the Spirit." (2 Cor 3:18)

It is this faith in a life of glory with Christ that keeps us growing here below. It is this faith that sustains us when we remember that "unless a grain of wheat falls to the ground and dies, it remains just a grain of wheat; but if it dies, it produces much fruit." (Jn 12:24) We can't skip over Good Friday to get to the Resurrection. We must patiently wait for the light that dispels all darkness. In the gift of Jesus in the Eucharist, we have the hidden seed of the Risen Lord in its entirety. We have the flicker of light that will become dazzling in the sunshine of Paradise, in the presence of God.

2. The Ascension

In order to keep the hope of Heaven in us and make it more efficacious, in order to have us wait patiently for the Heaven of glory and lead us there, our Lord has created the beautiful Heaven of the Eucharist. For the Eucharist is a beautiful Heaven; it is Heaven begun. Is it not Jesus glorified coming from Heaven to earth, and bringing Heaven with Him? Is not Heaven wherever our Lord is? His state there, although hidden from our senses, is one of glory, triumph, and blessedness. He has done away with the miseries of this life; when we go to Communion, we receive Heaven, since we receive Jesus Who is the whole joy and glory of Paradise.

Through Communion his soul ascends to God. Prayer is defined as an ascension of the soul to God. But what is prayer compared to Communion? What a difference between the ascension of our thoughts and desires in prayer and the sacramental ascension wherein Jesus raises us Himself to the very bosom of God![65]

---

[65] Eymard, *The Real Presence*, 286

75

Arise

The mystery of the Ascension speaks to us of hope, the hope of Heaven. "And if I go and prepare a place for you, I will come back again and take you to myself, so that where I am you also may be." (Jn 14:3) These words from Jesus can be applied to the Eucharist, as He, "in order to keep the hope of Heaven in us, has created the beautiful Heaven of the Eucharist."[66]

In Communion, Jesus comes down to us. Love seeks His beloved. He knocks on the door and finding a contrite heart, a garden enclosed, in which to make His home, He lifts us up to Himself, "to the very bosom of God."[67] In the Eucharist, we find all the sweetness and delights of Heaven, for Heaven is where Jesus is. We get a taste of Heaven and it leaves us wanting more. Our desire grows along with our hope each time we hear our lover speak and say to us, "Arise, my friend, my beautiful one, and come!" (Song 2:10)

---

[66] Eymard, *The Real Presence*, 286
[67] Ibid.,286

The Eucharistic presence of Christ endures as long as the Eucharistic species subsist (CCC, 1377), which is generally assumed to be around 10-15 minutes after receiving Communion.[68] Let us keep this reality before our eyes each time we receive Him. Let us give Him our whole hearts and minds for those precious minutes that the species are still in our bodies and we have Him, all glorious and immortal, with us. Let us let our minds and hearts ascend to Him like incense in the Heaven of the Eucharist as we patiently wait for Him to bring us with Him to the Heaven of glory.

[68] https://www.rcdop.org.uk/news/how-long-is-jesus-present-in-the-eucharist-after-weve-received-communion

3. The Coming of the Holy Spirit

God is all love. This gentle Savior pleads with us from the Host: 'Love Me as I have loved you; abide in My love! I came to cast the fire of love on the earth, and My most ardent desire is that it should set your hearts on fire.' Oh! What shall we think of the Eucharist at the moment of death or after death, when we shall see and know all the goodness and love and riches of it! [69]

---

[69] Eymard, *The Real Presence*, 154

Open to Me

The mystery of the Coming of the Holy Spirit speaks to us of the love of God. The Holy Spirit, loud as a mighty wind, descended upon the Apostles and upon Our Lady in the form of tongues of fire. He doesn't always make so much noise when He comes. This is the same Holy Spirit who during Mass quietly transforms the bread and wine into the Body and Blood of Our Lord, and comes gently into our hearts to set them on fire with the love of God.

The action of the Holy Spirit during Mass is quiet and gentle, like the dewfall. That moment when, through the ministry of the priest, the Holy Spirit changes the gifts human hands have made into the Body and Blood of our Lord Jesus Christ, is almost too elusive for our senses. Just like the precise moment the sunrise gives way to the fullness of light, the coming of the Holy Spirit gives way to His full power and action. This quiet and gentle Presence brings the fire of God's love with Him because He IS God's love Himself.

In one of the Eucharistic Prayers we hear the priest say the words, "Make holy, therefore, these gifts, we pray, by sending down your Spirit upon them like the dewfall..."[70] Once Jesus is present on the altar we can almost hear Him speaking to our hearts: "Open to me, my sister, my friend, my dove, my perfect one! For my head is wet with dew." (Song 5:2) He brings the dew of the Holy Spirit with Him in the Eucharist and knocks at the door of our hearts. He wants to fill us with His love.

How can we welcome such a guest? We can unite our prayers to the priest's and ask the Father to send His Holy Spirit upon us to transform us and make us holy; to make us a fitting dwelling for His Son. Thus, when we receive Jesus in the Eucharist we can let His Love fulfill his most ardent desire, to penetrate deeply into every recess of our beings and set our hearts on fire.

---

[70] Eucharistic Prayer II (http://www.catholic-resources.org/ChurchDocs/RM3-EP1-4.htm)

4. The Assumption of Mary

*Mary died of love. The longing to see her Son, and to be fully
united to Him, snapped her thread of life. Jesus is about to accord
her a grand triumph. O what passed between Jesus and Mary at
the moment of their meeting! We know the joy of a mother and
a son meeting after a long separation.* [71]

*In Communion we receive an unfailing pledge of immortality.
'He that eats my flesh, and drinks my blood, has everlasting'
eternal life. We lose our temporal life. But it is not a life worthy
of the name; it is only a halt on the journey to true life.* [72]

---

[71] Eymard, *Our Lady of the Most Blessed Sacrament*, 166
[72] Eymard, *The Real Presence*, 242

Trust Me

The mystery of the Assumption of Mary speaks to us of the resurrection of the body. "The Assumption of the Blessed Virgin is a singular participation in her Son's Resurrection and an anticipation of the resurrection of other Christians." (CCC, 968) Just like Mary has been taken up into Heaven body and soul, we live in the hope of the Resurrection, in that "unfailing pledge of immortality"[73] we receive in Communion.

In the book *Our Lady of the Most Blessed Sacrament*, St. Peter Julian explores the life of Mary in the Cenacle in the early years of the Church. He writes: "The Eucharist had so powerful an attraction for the Blessed Virgin that she could not live away from It."[74] It is sometimes hard to imagine that Our Lady's love for Jesus could grow even more than when she stood at the foot of the Cross, but we have to remember that love, being from God, if nurtured, can always grow. Mary's love for Jesus, nurtured by Holy

---

[73] Eymard, *The Real Presence*, 242
[74] Eymard, *Our Lady of the Most Blessed Sacrament*, 14

Communion and Adoration, grew until her longing snapped her thread of life and she died of love. [75]

When we meditate on our Mother being taken up into Heaven, into the loving arms of the Father, and reunited with her Son, we are filled with hope. She is always our Mother, and as such, she is interceding for us, and she is teaching and encouraging us. Let us then imitate her, remaining close to Jesus in the Most Blessed Sacrament. Let us receive Him often with great love and adore Him in the Tabernacle. Let us see His Body, glorious but hidden in the Host, and remember that He wants to sow the seed of His own Life in us, and raise us with Him on the last day.

---

[75] Eymard, *Our Lady of the Most Blessed Sacrament*, 166

5. The Coronation of Mary

Jesus led His Mother by the hand up to the throne of God. 'Behold, O Father, her with whom You are associated, by choosing her to give Me My Humanity!' —And the Father crowned her with her three most beautiful titles, Queen, Mother, Mediatrix. In Mary's diadem, three pearls are shining with dazzling brightness, namely, that of her humility, that of her poverty, and that of her sufferings. [76]

The tendency of love, its final tendency, is the union of two beings who love each other, the fusion of two into one, of two hearts into one heart, of two minds into one mind, of two souls into one soul. ...We abide in Him, He abides in us. We are one with Him until the ineffable union that was begun here below by grace and perfected by the Eucharist is consummated in Heaven in an eternal and glorious union. Love lives therefore with Jesus present in the Most Blessed Sacrament. It shares all that belongs to Jesus. It is one with Jesus. The demands of our heart are satisfied; it cannot ask for anything else. [77]

---

[76] Eymard, *Our Lady of The Blessed Sacrament*, 167
[77] Eymard, *The Real Presence*, 78

Let Go

The mystery of the Coronation of Mary speaks to us of eternal happiness. At the end of her earthly life, God gave Mary her reward: she will forever remain by her Son as Queen of Heaven and Earth. When we receive and adore Jesus in the Blessed Sacrament in the company of Mary, we have with us a Mother, Queen, and Mediatrix, who will always lead us to Christ. "Mary, the exalted Daughter of Sion, helps all her children, wherever they may be and whatever their condition, to find in Christ the path to the Father's house." [78] This path to Heaven is found in the Eucharist, where love lives, and fulfills all the desires of our hearts.

Mary's diadems' "three dazzling pearls" [79] shine for us to see and imitate, as they light up the way for us to follow. The first two reflect the virtues of Our Lord's poverty and humility in the Eucharist, and the third one, that of her sufferings, reminds us that she shares so closely in His glory now in Heaven because she shared so closely in His

---

[78] St. John Paul II, *"Redemptoris Mater,"* 47
[79] Eymard, *Our Lady of The Blessed Sacrament,* 167

sufferings on earth. We can see that these pearls do not shine on their own, but reflect the light from the Monstrance. In that Monstrance is Jesus in the Most Blessed Sacrament, the One we have been looking for, the One who will satisfy the demands of our hearts.

It is there our quest must end. "When he finds a pearl of great price, he goes and sells all that he has and buys it." (Mt 13:46) We must let go of anything that divides our hearts, for the price of this pearl is our whole hearts. Love dwelling in the Blessed Sacrament calls, "Arise, my friend, my beautiful one, and come!" (Song 2:10), for the final tendency of love is the union of two souls. This union "perfected by the Eucharist"[80] will satisfy our hearts until that final day when we say, "Before I knew it, my desire had made me the blessed one of the prince's people." (Song 6:12)

---

[80] Eymard, *The Real Presence*, 78

Acknowledgments

My heart is full of gratitude and joy for the many people who have helped me in one way or another to bring the idea of this book into reality. I would like to begin by thanking my dear friend Laura Worhacz for reading each draft of each reflection and for challenging me when she felt I could go deeper. Her friendship and support were, and still are, a great gift. I am grateful to Joan Alix for her invaluable advice in all aspects of formatting the book. With her help, what began as a plain manuscript ended up as a beautiful book. Special thanks to Andrew and Jennifer Whiskeyman for editing and proofreading, and to Jill Samuels for photographing my rosary for the cover. This rosary has special significance to me. It was a gift from my very good friends Dimitre and Theresa Bobev, who traveled to Fatima for the 100th anniversary celebration and prayed for me while they were there. I am especially grateful to Father William Fickel for his guidance, support and especially his constant encouragement throughout this project. His love for Jesus in the Blessed Sacrament and in His people are a continuous source of inspiration for me. Grateful to the Mothers of the Blessed Sacrament, for their faithful prayers for me and my family. They are always just an email away, ready to pray. I'd like to thank my son Carlos for taking my picture for the back cover and for his patient help getting my website up and running. To my other two sons, Gabriel and Miguel, I am grateful for their cheerful disposition anytime I needed to work on the book, and their help with the house and the dogs. Most of all, I am forever grateful to my husband, Rick, for the many hours discussing theology, sitting in Adoration, and attending daily Mass with me. For his listening heart when I felt overwhelmed or discouraged and his willingness to speak Truth to me always – for his kind smile when I went on and on about some aspect of this book -- for being my draft reader, first editor and theology consultant – for willingly embarking on this journey with me, for his love and support -- thank you. I am blessed.

About the Author

Ivonne J. Hernandez lives in Florida with her husband of twenty-six years and her children. She left her career as a computer engineer to become first a stay-at-home mom, and then a homeschooling mom. Two of her children have since graduated and she continues to homeschool her youngest son, now in high school, while working on different ministries. Ivonne and her husband are Lay Associates of the Congregation of the Blessed Sacrament, and work together to further the love of Jesus in the Eucharist. Ivonne is also a regular contributor for the Center for Eucharistic Evangelizing's Daily Eucharistic Reflection [81], and the Elisheba Blog. [82]

---

[81] http://www.eucharisticevangelizing.com
[82] http://www.elishebahouse.com/blog

References

Baltimore, P. a. (1885). *A Catechism of Christian Doctrine Book 1*. New York .

Eymard, S. P. (1930). *Our Lady of The Blessed Sacrament.* Cleveland, Ohio: Emmanuel Publications.

Eymard, S. P. (1938). *The Real Presence.* Cleveland, Ohio: Emmanuel Publishing.

Vaticana, L. E. (n.d.). *Catechism of the Catholic Church, second edition.* United States Conference of Catholic Bishops. Kindle Edition.

Printed in Great Britain
by Amazon